Face Off!

You Can Play Hockey

by *Nick Fauchald*
illustrated by *Ronnie Rooney*

Special thanks to our advisers for their expertise:

Jim Bugenhagen, Director of Hockey
Chelsea Piers–Sky Rink, New York, New York

Susan Kesselring, M.A., Literacy Educator
Rosemount–Apple Valley–Eagan (Minnesota) School District

Editorial Director: Carol Jones
Managing Editor: Catherine Neitge
Creative Director: Keith Griffin
Editor: Jill Kalz
Story Consultant: Terry Flaherty
Designer: Joe Anderson
Page Production: Picture Window Books
The illustrations in this book were created with acrylics.

Picture Window Books
5115 Excelsior Boulevard
Suite 232
Minneapolis, MN 55416
877-845-8392
www.picturewindowbooks.com

Printed in the United States of America.

Library of Congress Cataloging-in-Publication Data
Fauchald, Nick.
Face off! You can play hockey / by Nick Fauchald ; illustrated by Ronnie Rooney.
p. cm. — (Game day)
Includes bibliographical references and index.
ISBN 1-4048-1154-0 (hardcover)
1. Hockey—Juvenile literature. I. Title: Face off!. II. Title: You can play hockey. III. Rooney,
Ronnie. IV. Title.
GV847.25.F38 2006
796.962—dc22   2005004270

Hockey is a fun sport that can be played outdoors or indoors. It is one of the fastest games around. Kids all over the world play hockey. Let's go find some ice and play!

You get to the ice rink just in time for passing and shooting practice. Your team, the Penguins, is playing the Seals today. When the referee blows the whistle, the game will start.

Hockey is played at an ice rink. The large, flat floor is covered with smooth ice. Where it's cold in the winter, ice rinks can be made outside. Some people even play hockey on frozen lakes.

To start the game, the Penguins and the Seals meet at center ice for a face-off. The referee drops a small rubber disk, called a puck, between one player from each team. Your team wins the face-off to get control of the puck.

You need lots of equipment to play hockey. A helmet and special pads protect you from the hard ice. A hockey stick is used to pass and shoot the puck. Most important are ice skates—special boots with metal blades on the bottom. You use skates to move across the ice.

7

Tom skates with the puck toward the Seals'
net. He passes to Anna. She shoots and misses.

*The object of hockey is to shoot the puck into
the other team's net. A successful shot is
called making a goal. Each game is
divided into three 20-minute periods.
The team with the most goals at the end
of the game wins.*

The Seals now have the puck. They pass it back and forth as they move toward your goal. You skate toward the player with the puck and steal it away with your hockey stick.

The team that controls the puck is on offense. Its mission is to score goals. The other team, called the defense, tries to steal the puck and stop the offense from scoring.

Each team has a goalie, a special player who stays in front of the net and tries to block shots. The goalie wears extra pads and uses a bigger stick and a glove to help stop the puck.

You skate past center ice and pass the puck to Cameron, but a Seal steals it. He has an open path to the net. He winds up for a shot. The puck flies right at the goalie, but she blocks it.

The game moves fast. Both teams skate back and forth on the ice. They pass. They shoot.

Higher-level hockey players sometimes use their bodies to try to steal the puck from an opponent or to slow their opponent down. This move is called body checking. You can only do this to a player who has the puck.

The goalies do a good job of
keeping the puck out of the nets.

There are two main kinds of shots: the wrist shot and the slap shot. To shoot a wrist shot, keep your stick on the ground and quickly flick the puck toward the net. To shoot a slap shot, swing the stick back quickly then forward to "slap" the puck ahead.

It's near the end of the third period. The score is still
tied, 0-0. The Seals get the puck and move toward the
Penguins' net. Your teammate Britta steals the puck
from the Seals and begins to skate to the other end of
the rink.

Britta passes to Cameron, who skates around the Seals' defense. You skate toward the net to get open for a pass. Cameron sees you and passes the puck.

If you slash, trip, or high-stick another player (use your stick to hit), the referee will call a penalty on you. You'll have to leave the ice and sit in the penalty box.

19

Only the goalie is between you and the net. You wind up and take a shot. The puck sails past the goalie and into the net. Goal! The Penguins win!

You and all the other players line up on the ice and slap hands. Both teams played a great game!

Diagram of a Hockey Rink

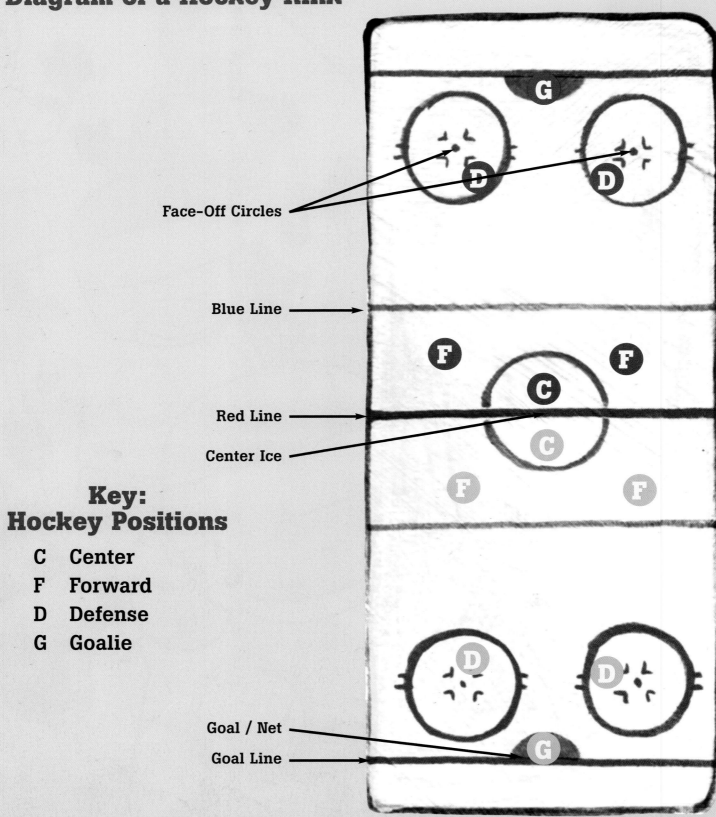

Face-Off Circles

Blue Line

Red Line

Center Ice

Key:
Hockey Positions

C Center
F Forward
D Defense
G Goalie

Goal / Net

Goal Line

FUN FACTS

 In the 1800s, people throughout Canada and northern Europe played an early form of hockey known by many names, including "shinny" and "shinty." Players used tree branches to push stones across the ice.

 The National Hockey League (NHL) was started in November 1917. It is a group of professional hockey teams from the United States and Canada. There are currently 30 teams in the NHL.

 Women's hockey became an official Olympic sport in the 1998 Winter Games in Nagano, Japan. Of the six teams that competed, the United States won the gold medal, and Canada won the silver.

 Some NHL teams use up to 5,000 pucks in a single season. Pucks are frozen before games. The hard, frozen rubber helps the puck slide better and bounce less.

 Wayne Gretzky holds the record for most career goals (894 goals in 1,487 games).

GLOSSARY

face-off—when the referee drops the puck between one player from each team; a face-off is used to start play at the beginning of the game and after play has been stopped

penalty—punishment a player gets when he or she breaks a rule of the game; the player then has to sit in the penalty box for two or more minutes

slap shot—the fastest and most forceful shot in the game; a player raises his or her stick and slaps the puck hard toward the goal, putting his or her full body power behind it

slash—to swing at another player with a stick

wrist shot—a type of shot in which a player uses his or her wrists to quickly snap the stick and shoot the puck

TO LEARN MORE

At the Library

Ayers, Tom. *The Illustrated Rules of Ice Hockey*. Nashville: Ideals Children's Books, 1995.

Ditchfield, Christin. *Ice Hockey*. New York: Children's Press, 2003.

Thomas, Keltie. *How Hockey Works: The Science of Hockey*. Toronto: Maple Tree Press, 2002.

Wilson, Stacy. *The Hockey Book for Girls*. Toronto: Kids Can Press, 2000.

On the Web

FactHound offers a safe, fun way to find Web sites related to this book.
All of the sites on FactHound have been researched by our staff.
http://www.facthound.com

1. Visit the FactHound home page.
2. Enter a search word related to this book,
   or type in this special code: 1404811540.
3. Click on the FETCH IT button.

Your trusty FactHound will fetch the best sites for you!

INDEX

body checking, 14

face-off, 6, 22

goalie, 12, 13, 15, 20, 22

Gretzky, Wayne, 23

hockey stick, 6, 10, 12, 16, 19

ice rink, 4, 5, 17

ice skates, 6

National Hockey League (NHL), 23

Olympic sport, 23

penalty, 19

scoring, 11, 17

shooting, 4, 6, 9, 14, 16

Look for all the books in the Game Day series:

Batter Up! You Can Play Softball

Bump! Set! Spike! You Can Play Volleyball

Face Off! You Can Play Hockey

Jump Ball! You Can Play Basketball

Nice Hit! You Can Play Baseball

Score! You Can Play Soccer

Tee Off! You Can Play Golf

Touchdown! You Can Play Football